WITHDRAWN

Physical Science
Sound

JOSH GREGORY

Children's Press®
An Imprint of Scholastic Inc.

Content Consultant
Valarie Akerson, PhD, Professor of Science Education
Department of Curriculum and Instruction
Indiana University Bloomington, Bloomington, Indiana

Library of Congress Cataloging-in-Publication Data
Names: Gregory, Josh, author.
Title: Sound / by Josh Gregory.
Description: New York, NY : Scholastic Inc., 2019. | Series: A true book | Includes bibliographical
    references and index.
Identifiers: LCCN 2018034482| ISBN 9780531131428 (library binding) | ISBN 9780531136058 (pbk.)
Subjects: LCSH: Sound—Juvenile literature.
Classification: LCC QC225.5 .G75 2019 | DDC 534—dc23
LC record available at https://lccn.loc.gov/2018034482

All rights reserved. Published in 2019 by Children's Press, an imprint of Scholastic Inc.
Printed in North Mankato, MN, USA 113

SCHOLASTIC, CHILDREN'S PRESS, A TRUE BOOK™, and associated logos are trademarks and/or
registered trademarks of Scholastic Inc.

Scholastic Inc., 557 Broadway, New York, NY 10012

1 2 3 4 5 6 7 8 9 10 R 28 27 26 25 24 23 22 21 20 19

Front cover: A child yelling into a megaphone
**Back cover: Musicians playing in
a human-made bubble**

Find the Truth!

Everything you are about to read is true *except* for one of the sentences on this page.

Which one is **TRUE**?

T or F   Sound moves faster than light does.

T or F   It is very quiet in outer space.

Find the answers in this book.

Contents

THE BIG TRUTH!

How We Hear

3 Make Some Noise

The trumpet's shape
affects its sound.

People can listen to music played by their cell phones.

4 On the Record

How are sound recordings made?............... **35**

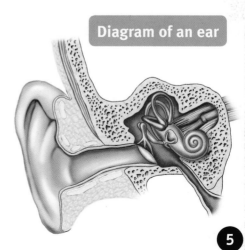

Diagram of an ear

Think About It!

Look closely at the photo on these pages. What type of place does the image show? What sounds do you think would be heard here? What do you see in the image that makes you think you'd hear those sounds? How would these sounds be different from the sounds heard in other places, such as mountaintops, small towns, or outer space?

Intrigued?
Want to know more? Turn the page!

What sounds do you imagine could be heard in a scene like this one?

Sound Everywhere

A busy city street is full of sounds. Cars on the street have roaring engines and honking horns. Footsteps and talking come from people walking by. There is a construction crew using loud, heavy machines. Music drifts by from nearby windows.

Outside the city, sounds still surround you. Leaves rustle in the breeze and songbirds call to one another. You hear your footsteps and your clothing rubbing against itself. You even notice your own breathing.

Even though we can't see it, sound is all around us, all the time. We can hear it, and sometimes we can even feel it. It gives us information about what is going on around us, and we can use it to communicate. But what exactly is sound? Put simply, sounds are vibrations in the air. But there is much more to it than that.

Experts carefully design sound systems to make the music sound just right at a concert.

The ear contains the smallest bones in the entire human body.

You can make a "telephone" with two cans and some string.

CHAPTER 1

Good Vibrations

Sound is a form of energy. In science, **energy** is the ability to perform work. Energy can take many forms in addition to sound, including heat, light, and electricity. It can be transferred from one object to another. It can also be changed from one form to another. Energy can never, however, be created or destroyed. This means sound is never created from nothing, and it never simply disappears. It always comes from other energy, and it can become other kinds of energy.

A guitar's sound comes from the vibration of its strings.

Moving Through a Medium

Sound energy moves through a **medium** as vibrations. Usually, the medium is air or a liquid. Sometimes it's a solid object. The vibration jostles **particles** of **matter** in the medium. The particles move and bump into the particles next to them. These particles bump into other particles, which bump into more particles, and so on. This is how sound travels.

Sound cannot move through a **vacuum**. A vacuum is an area empty of matter. Sound has no particles to hit. For example, outer space is a vacuum. Sounds cannot be heard there.

Sounds are always moving. Sometimes they vibrate out in all directions from a central point. Think about the sound of hands clapping in applause. Other times, sounds are aimed in a specific direction. This is how headphones work.

A sound's speed depends on the medium it is traveling through. Sound moves faster through water than through air. Water particles are closer together. As a result, the vibration bumps from one particle to the next much faster.

Sound does not travel as fast as light does. This is why you can see lightning before you hear the sound it makes—thunder.

Some headphones are designed not only to play music, but also to block other sounds.

A soft, textured material such as foam is better at absorbing sound than a hard, flat one. Foam often lines the walls of recording studios like this one.

When Sound Meets Matter

As sound vibrations move, they are changed by the matter they run into. When sound waves hit a wall or other solid object, they are partially absorbed and turned into heat energy. The remaining waves keep moving past the wall, but now they sound different. This is why sounds seem muffled or **distorted** when heard from another room.

Sounds can also affect and change one another if they move through the same medium. This is called interference.

Echo Echo

When a sound hits a hard object, some vibrations bounce and are sent back the way they came. This is what causes an echo. You are most likely to hear an echo somewhere with very hard, smooth walls and few other objects that can absorb sound. This is why echoes are common in empty rooms, caves, and canyons.

In some watery caves, the sound of water hitting the cave's sides creates a constant echo.

Creating a Sound

Sounds are formed when some other type of energy creates a vibration. For example, think about what happens when you clap your hands. The air between your hands is suddenly forced to move as your hands come together. This begins a sound vibration. So does the vibration of your hands as they hit each other. Try waving your hand in the air near your ear. You can probably hear the air whooshing around as you move.

You don't only hear the vibration of a clap. You can also feel it.

In return, sounds can also make matter vibrate. This effect is called **resonance**. To experience it yourself, turn on some music at a loud (but safe) volume. Now put your hand very close to the speaker. If the music is loud enough, you should be able to feel the vibrations in your hand. In extremely loud environments, such as concerts, sounds can even make the floor and walls shake.

A tuning fork often vibrates too slightly for you to see it. Dip the fork in water, however, and you can see the effect those vibrations have on the liquid.

Ocean waves and sound waves both carry energy.

Waves that curl over into a "tube" shape create a different sound than other waves when they crash against the shore.

CHAPTER 2

Ride the Wave

Sound vibrations take a shape called a wave. You have probably seen ocean waves or the circular ripples caused by dropping something into a liquid. While these aren't sound waves, they work much the same way. As waves spread out from their source, they move up and down in a repeating pattern. Waves vary in size and speed. These characteristics affect what you hear when a sound wave reaches you.

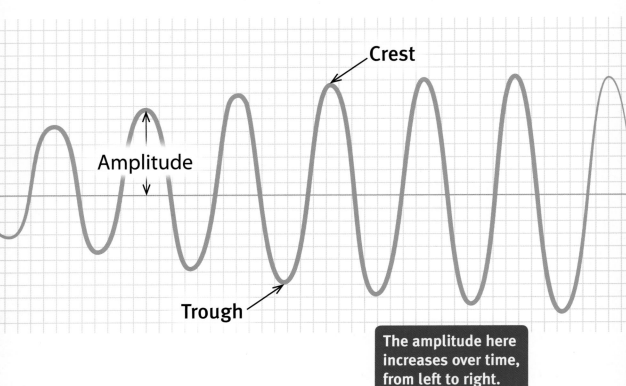

Crest

Amplitude

Trough

The amplitude here increases over time, from left to right.

Amplitude

There are several ways to measure the differences between sound waves. One is called **amplitude**. Take a look at the sound wave diagram above. The highest point of a sound wave is called its crest. The lowest point is the trough. Amplitude is measured as half of the distance between these two points.

The amplitude of a sound wave determines its volume. Loud sounds have high crests and low troughs. Their waves look like tall mountains with deep valleys between them. Quieter sound waves look more like gently rolling hills.

Amplitude is measured in units called decibels (dB). The sound of leaves blowing in the wind has a volume of about 10 dB. A jet airplane, on the other hand, produces about 120 dB as it takes off.

Plane engines are loud. People working on the ground at airports wear special earplugs or earmuffs to protect their hearing.

Frequency

Another important measurement is called **frequency**. Frequency describes how quickly a sound wave is moving. It is measured by the number of times a wave moves through a single point in its pattern within one second. This might be anywhere from just a few times per second to tens of thousands of times per second.

Opera singers sing different notes by controlling the frequency of their voices.

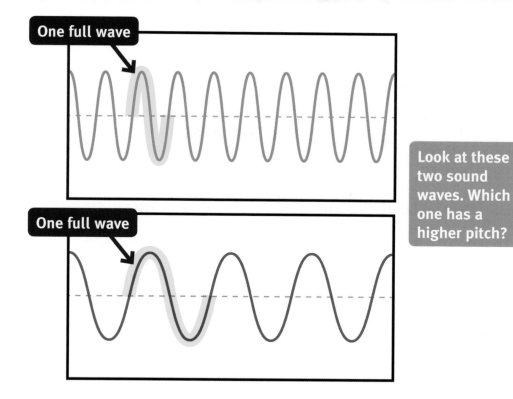

One full wave

One full wave

Look at these two sound waves. Which one has a higher pitch?

The unit of measurement for frequency is hertz (hz). A sound with 1 hz completes one full wave every second. Most sounds, however, move much faster than that.

A sound wave's frequency affects its **pitch**. The lower the frequency of a sound wave, the lower its pitch will sound, like the boom of a bass drum. High-frequency waves produce high-pitched sounds, like those of a flute.

Wavelength

Wavelength is a measurement that is very closely related to frequency. It is usually measured as the distance from one crest to the next, or from one trough to the next. Waves with high frequencies are closer together, so they have short wavelengths. Waves with low frequencies are stretched out. They have long wavelengths.

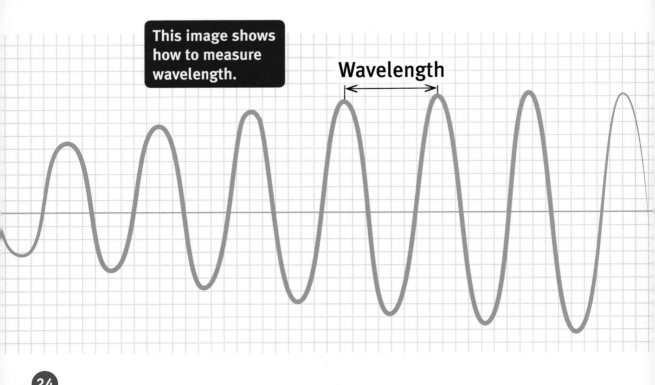

This image shows how to measure wavelength.

Wavelength

Waves in Motion

Waves **contract** and stretch as the source of the sound moves closer to or farther from your ear. This changes the sound's wavelength and frequency. This is why you hear a *whoosh* as a car drives by, and why the sound of a siren changes as a police car passes by. First, the sound's pitch goes higher as the siren moves toward you. This is because the wavelength is becoming shorter. Then, as the siren moves away, the pitch drops. This is the wavelength stretching out. This change in sound is called the Doppler effect.

People in the seats at NASCAR races experience the Doppler effect as cars speed by.

DIAGRAM OF DOPPLER EFFECT

Moving object

Sound waves stretched behind

Sound waves compressed in front

Still object

Sound waves unchanged and even

How We Hear

Hearing is our ability to notice sound waves and turn them into useful information. The process begins with our ears. This is how it works:

1 The outer ear is shaped to collect sound waves from the air.

2 Sound waves are then funneled toward the eardrum. This is a thin, tightly stretched piece of skin. When sound waves hit it, it vibrates.

3 The vibrations move farther inside the ear to the cochlea. It changes the vibrations to electrical signals.

Outer Ear

4 The electrical signals travel through **nerves** to the brain.

5 The brain determines the pitch, volume, and other qualities of the sound.

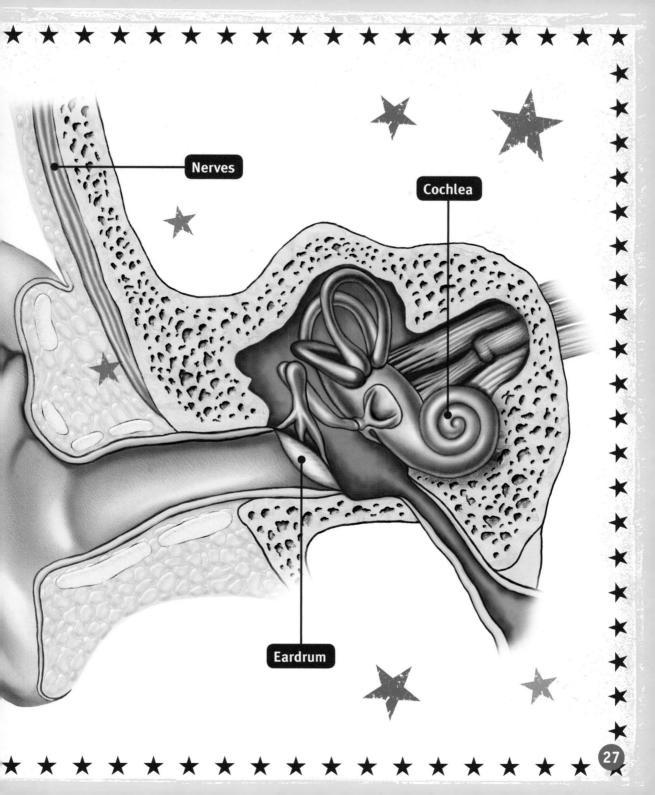

Nerves

Cochlea

Eardrum

Humans hear sounds from roughly 20 hz to 20,000 hz. The greater wax moth hears sounds of up to 300,000 hz.

Actors on stage often use microphones to make sure everyone in the audience can hear them. In some cases, the shape of the theater is designed to help sounds travel.

CHAPTER 3

Make Some Noise

People use sound in an incredible variety of ways. Most people rely on it to communicate with one another. Sound lets us know when cars or other objects are approaching from outside our view. It can also be used to create beautiful music. Believe it or not, people have even found uses for sound waves that don't involve hearing at all.

A Way With Words

People most often make sounds by talking. Inside your throat is a tube called a larynx. The larynx contains your vocal cords. These bands of tissue vibrate when your breath passes over them. Their vibrations create sound waves. You control the pitch of the sound waves by tightening or loosening your vocal cords. As your voice makes its way out of your mouth, you form the sound into words by moving your tongue and lips.

A person's voice (the yellow arrow) travels up through the larynx and out through the mouth.

Vocal cords

Sounds such as the wind in the trees and nearby birds can be heard through this human-made bubble, so they add to the sounds of the musicians inside the bubble.

Playing a Tune

Musical instruments produce sound waves at a range of frequencies. Different instruments produce vibrations in different ways. String instruments, such as guitars, have vibrating strings. Trumpets and other brass instruments use vibrations from the player's lips. The instruments shape these vibrations into various sounds. With woodwind instruments, such as clarinets, players blow across a thin strip of material called a reed, which vibrates. Percussion instruments, such as drums, vibrate when they are struck.

31

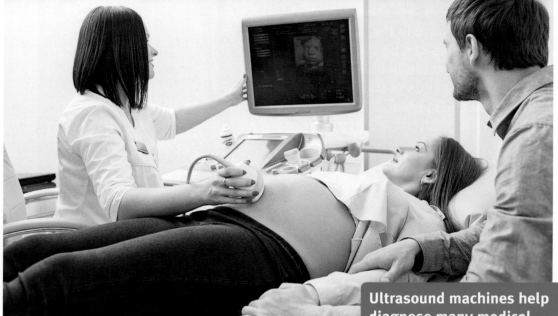

Ultrasound machines help diagnose many medical issues and observe fetuses developing in a mother's belly.

Scanning With Sound

Sound waves are a safe and painless way to see inside the human body. An ultrasound machine produces sound at a frequency beyond what people can hear. These sound waves are aimed at a person's body. They easily pass through skin, blood, and other body materials. Denser body parts, such as organs and bones, partially reflect the sound waves back. The reflected waves are recorded and used to make an image of the body's interior.

Underwater Waves

Similarly, sound waves can be used to explore and map underwater areas. Sonar (SOund Navigation And Ranging) systems send sound waves through the water. The waves bounce off of solid objects and return to the sonar system. By measuring how long it took the wave to return, the system can determine how far away the object is. If the object is in motion, a sonar system can also figure out its speed and direction.

Dolphins, bats, and certain other animals have built-in sonar systems called echolocation. They use it to navigate and search for food.

This diagram shows a dolphin using echolocation to hunt a fish.

In animated films, all the sounds have to be created by humans, from voices to footsteps.

Actress Miranda Cosgrove stands in the sound booth to record her voice for the animated film *Despicable Me*.

CHAPTER 4

On the Record

There are some sounds we want to hear over and over, like a favorite song or a moving speech. Perhaps you enjoy the rumbling sound effects in a movie. Or maybe you'd like to leave a voice message for a friend to hear later. Thanks to sound recording technology, these activities are no trouble at all. The first known sound recording was made in 1857. Since then, recorded sound has become a common part of life for most people.

Capturing a Wave

There are several ways to record sound waves. The most common method involves electricity. First, a sound is captured with a microphone. The microphone converts, or changes, it into an electrical wave with the same shape as the sound wave. The shape of the electrical wave can then be "written" onto different materials. For example, records are made by cutting the wave's shape into a disc of plastic material called vinyl.

Timeline of Sound Through the Ages

About 40,000 BCE
People create the earliest known musical instruments.

1876
Alexander Graham Bell makes the world's first telephone call.

About 40,000 BCE > **1857 CE** > **1876** > **1877**

1857 CE
French inventor Édouard-Léon Scott de Martinville creates the first known sound recording (left). There is still no way to play the recording.

1877
Thomas Edison invents the phonograph, the first device to both record and play back sounds.

Digital Recordings

Most sound recordings today are digital. This means they are not physical materials, but computer files. After a microphone converts a sound wave to an electrical wave, a computer converts the wave into a complex pattern of 1s and 0s. This is called **binary code**, and it is how computers "think." Every time a computer reads a certain pattern of binary code, it can reproduce the recording's exact original electronic wave.

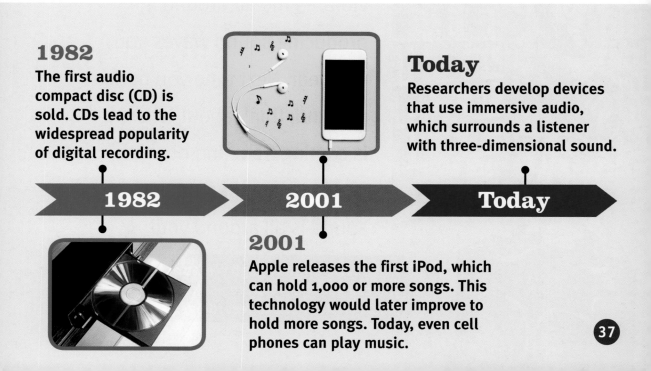

1982
The first audio compact disc (CD) is sold. CDs lead to the widespread popularity of digital recording.

Today
Researchers develop devices that use immersive audio, which surrounds a listener with three-dimensional sound.

| 1982 | 2001 | Today |

2001
Apple releases the first iPod, which can hold 1,000 or more songs. This technology would later improve to hold more songs. Today, even cell phones can play music.

Pushing the Air

A sound recording isn't much use without some way to play it back. First, a device such as a computer or smartphone converts the recording back into an electrical wave. This is sent to one or more speakers. The wave vibrates a device called a driver. The driver's vibrations move into a layer of thin, flexible material called a cone. The cone vibrates the air around it, producing sound waves you can hear. Next time you notice a sound, think about where it is coming from and how it is reaching you. Remember: sound is all around you!

If you have large enough stereo speakers, you can see them vibrate as they play music or other sound recordings.

Careers in Sound

Are you interested in sound or recording? If so, one of these careers might be for you!

Recording engineers operate recording equipment at a studio and help clients mix different sounds into a single recording.

Live audio engineers make sure voices and instruments are mixed together so they can all be heard. They control the overall volume during live performances.

Musicians are experts at playing their instruments to produce the exact sounds they want to hear.

Audiologists are experts who specialize in hearing. They often help patients recover from hearing loss and other hearing-related disorders.

Acoustic consultants help plan the design and construction of theaters and other spaces to help sound travel through them properly.

Make Your Own Record Player

Build your own record player to play musical sound waves without any electricity.

Materials

- ☐ Sharpened pencil
- ☐ Vinyl record (Make sure it's one that you don't mind damaging.)
- ☐ Clear tape
- ☐ Sheet of notebook or printer paper
- ☐ Metal sewing needle (Ask an adult for help)

Directions

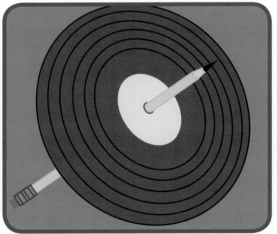

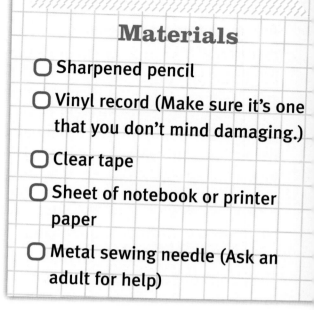

1. Stick the pencil through the hole in the center of the record. Make sure the pencil's tip sticks a couple of inches out the other side. Tape it in place.

2. Roll up the paper to form a cone shape. Tape it together.

3. Stick the needle sideways through the end of the cone, about 0.5 inch from the tip. Make sure it sticks through both sides of the cone.

4. Have a friend twirl the pencil on a flat surface to make the record spin. Gently set the cone's needle so it rests on the record. While holding the cone still, put your ear up to the open end. Can you hear the music?

5. Ask your friend to spin the record faster and slower. What happens to the music?

Explain It!

Using what you learned in this book, why do you think the speed of the record changes the sound? If you need help, turn back to pages 22 and 23 for more information.

Sound in Motion

What does the Doppler effect sound like? Try this experiment to find out.

Directions

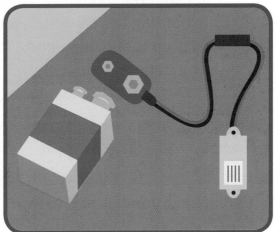

1. Connect the battery to the buzzer. Ask an adult if you need help. It should start buzzing once it is connected.

2. Ask an adult to cut an opening in the ball with the knife. Fill most of the ball with wadded-up paper. Place the buzzer and battery inside the ball. The paper will keep the buzzer from bouncing around.

3. Tape the ball shut securely. Make sure you can still hear the buzzer clearly. If you can't hear it, make sure the battery is connected. You might also try using less tape.

4. Stand in one place and ask two people to stand 10 feet to either side. Have them throw the ball back and forth. You should hear the sound of the buzzer as the ball goes past you. What happens to the sound as it moves closer or farther away?

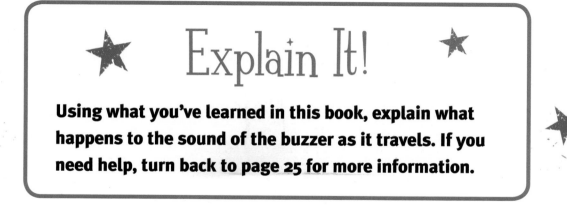

Explain It!

Using what you've learned in this book, explain what happens to the sound of the buzzer as it travels. If you need help, turn back to page 25 for more information.

Average range of frequencies that a human can hear: 20 to 20,000 hz

Average frequency range of a dog's hearing: 67 to 45,000 hz

Average frequency range of a dolphin's hearing: 90 to 105,000 hz

Average volume of human speech: 45 to 60 dB

Average volume of a rock concert: 110 dB

Volume at which sounds start to become unpleasant for most people: 90 dB

Volume at which sounds can cause serious hearing loss: 120 dB

Did you find the truth?

(**F**) Sound moves faster than light does.

(**T**) It is very quiet in outer space.

Resources

Books

Kenney, Karen Latchana. *Sound and Light Waves Investigations*. Minneapolis: Lerner Publications, 2018.

Midthun, Joseph, and Samuel Hiti. *Sound*. Chicago: World Book, 2012.

Winterberg, Jenna. *Sound Waves and Communication*. Huntington Beach, CA: Teacher Created Materials, 2016.

Visit this Scholastic website for more information on sound:
★ www.factsfornow.scholastic.com
Enter the keyword **Sound**

Important Words

amplitude (AM-plih-tood) a measurement of the height of a sound wave

binary code (BYE-nur-ee KODE) the two-digit code computers use to process data

contract (kuhn-TRAKT) to become smaller

distorted (dih-STORT-id) altered or twisted out of shape

energy (EN-ur-jee) the ability of something to do work

frequency (FREE-kwuhn-see) the speed with which a sound wave moves, measured in cycles per second

matter (MAT-ur) something that has weight and takes up space

medium (MEE-dee-uhm) an intervening substance through which something else is transmitted or carried on

nerves (NURVZ) the bundles of fibers that send messages between the brain and other parts of the body so a person can move and feel

particles (PAHR-tih-kuhlz) extremely small pieces or amounts of something

pitch (PICH) the highness or lowness of a sound

resonance (REZ-uh-nehns) the vibration of a mechanical or electrical system caused by sound waves with a large amplitude

vacuum (VAK-yoom) a space that is empty of matter

Index

Page numbers in **bold** indicate illustrations.

About the Author

Josh Gregory is the author of more than 125 books for young readers. He currently lives in Chicago, Illinois.